Tropical

Butterflies

of the World

J. Duane Sept

National Library of Canada Cataloguing in Publication

Sept, J. Duane, 1950-
    Tropical butterflies of the world / J. Duane Sept.

Includes bibliographical references and index.
ISBN 0-9730390-4-3

    1. Butterflies—Tropics—Identification. I. Title.

QL560.6.S46 2003   595.78'9'0913   C2004-900022-5

All Photos copyright © J. Duane Sept except as noted on p. 76.

Front Cover Photo: Tiger longwing by J. Duane Sept.
Back Cover Photos: Common glasswing & Doris longwing by J.
                Duane Sept.

Published by:
Calypso Publishing
P.O. Box 1141
Sechelt, BC Canada
V0N 3A0

Website: http://www.calypso-publishing.com

CONTENTS

INTRODUCTION

Fossil records indicate that the delightful butterfly has been present for at least 30 million years. Today, man finds these delicate wonders of the natural world as intriguing as ever. We marvel at the diverse colors ranging from darkest black to the brightest of reds and yellows. We are intrigued by butterfly flight whether it is rapid and direct or slow and moth-like, short in distance from flower to flower, or the migration of thousands of miles.

Butterflies and moths are insects that belong to the order LEPIDOPTERA, meaning scaled wings. The order Lepidoptera is divided into butterflies and moths. The butterfly subsection (Rhopalocera) is divided into two main superfamilies called true butterflies (Papilionoidea) and skippers (Hesperioidea). Scientists tell us there are only 12,000 to 20,000 species of butterflies and 120,000 to 150,000 species of moths.

Common Blue Morpho

Large tree nymph.

Butterfly or Moth

When you first begin to look at moths and butterflies you may not be able to tell them apart. But as you continue to study these winged jewels you will become better at distinguishing the characteristics that are generally used to separate them. Not all moth or butterfly species exhibit all characteristics.

With a few exceptions, the following characteristics generally distinguish butterflies from moths.

Butterflies

Orange-barred sulfur.

• have long, slender antennae with club-like tips;
• have long, slender bodies;
• have brightly colored wings;
• rest with wings above or lying flat;
• are diurnal (active in the day) or crepuscular (active at dusk and dawn);
• as larvae, have less hair than a moth;
• as pupae often hang from a branch or leaf without any covering, not even hair.

6

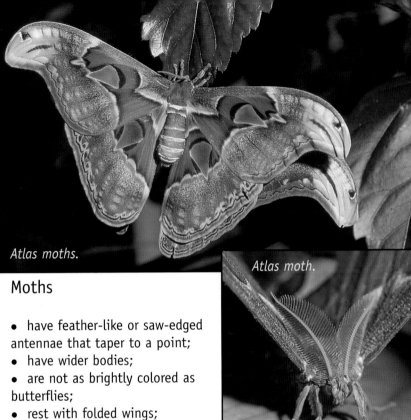

Atlas moths.

Atlas moth.

Moths

- have feather-like or saw-edged antennae that taper to a point;
- have wider bodies;
- are not as brightly colored as butterflies;
- rest with folded wings;
- are nocturnal (active at night);
- as larvae, have more hair than butterflies;
- transform into pupae that may be covered with a silky cocoon.

Atlas Moth

The atlas moth (*Attacus atlas*) of Southeast Asia has the largest wing surface of any moth in the world. No one knows the purpose of the transparent wing sections. We do know that when the wings are closed they look like a snake's head, eyes and all. They are believed to scare predators.

The adult atlas moth does not eat. It doesn't even have a mouth! It lives off body fat for two weeks.

The female produces powerful pheromones, a scent that attracts males from as far away as three miles downwind. If the female fails to attract a mate, and her eggs are unfertilized, she produces only males.

Tropical Butterflies

Butterflies can be divided into species living in tropical or temperate areas. Tropical butterflies live where there is a warm climate with an average temperature of 25° C (75° F) and no threat of freezing. Temperate species, however, live in cooler areas with the average temperature between 10° C and 13° C (50° F and 55° F). Only species living in temperate areas hibernate while many tropical species are active year-round.

This book focuses on those species that originate from tropical climates. The range of several of these species also includes some temperate areas.

A leafwing feeds on nectar.

Butterfly Foods

The larva of each butterfly species feeds on specific plants. Longwings, for example, feed on passion vine flowers (*Passiflora* spp.).

Golden helicons feed on pollen.

Adult butterflies, on the other hand, feed on a wide range of foods: Nectar is a common butterfly food around the world. Other foods for tropical butterfly species include ripe, fallen fruit, tree sap, dung, carrion, and rotting plant material. Adult longwings, for example, eat only pollen, giving them a nine-month lifespan, significantly longer than the average lifespan of adult butterflies, which is only ten days.

Behavior

Roosting

Butterflies busy searching for food and a mate while battling rivals, need an inconspicuous place to rest overnight and to avoid the danger of heavy rain. Most butterflies roost individually in various sheltered locations. Several species, from poisonous to edible, roost communally. For the edible species, it appears safety is found in numbers. We do not know why poisonous butterflies roost communally.

Puddling

Butterflies often gather in aggregations at puddles. Although scientists do not know all the reasons for this behavior, it is possible that the males, at least, are there for minerals, especially sodium, since the male transfers a large percentage of his sodium to the female in the spermatophore during mating.

Techniques for Survival

Camouflage

The better the camouflage, the better chance a species has for survival. Some butterflies resemble their surroundings and so do not draw attention to themselves. An adult may look like a

This swallowtail larva resembles a bird dropping.

dead leaf (see p. 45) while a caterpillar may look like a bird dropping (see above). As a result, predators are often unaware that a potential meal is nearby.

Mimicry

Poisonous butterflies send a warning signal to predators through their bright colors. Once a predator has had a taste of one of these butterflies it tends to stay away from others with similar colors. Some non-poisonous species take advantage of this and mimic the colors of their poisonous cousins. The mocker swallowtail (see p. 30) is one species that uses this ploy, called Batesian mimicry.

In another form of mimicry, called Mullerian mimicry, one or more poisonous species strongly resemble another poisonous species or model. The advantage is that a predator does not have to learn different warning colorations for each species. The postman (see p. 58) and small postman (see p. 60) take advantage of Mullerian mimicry.

Eyespots

Scientists believe large eyespots on butterflies startle or distract predators. Small eyespots, on the other hand, change the focus of an attack to an area of the butterfly that is not as important. For example, if a bird attacks a hindwing and focuses on the eyespot area thinking it is the head of an insect, it will harm the wing, rather than more crucial body parts of the butterfly.

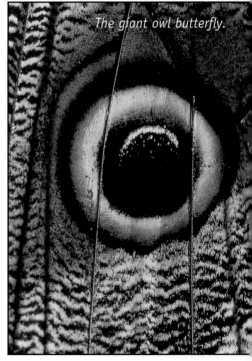

The giant owl butterfly.

Golden helicons mating.

Courtship and Mating

Butterflies have no time to linger over romance. They generally have only ten days in which to go from finding a mate to fertilizing and laying eggs on a suitable host plant.

Each sex has its own tools for finding a mate. Females use pheromones, chemicals with strongly attractive scents, to prepare and attract males from great distances. Males, on the other hand, rely on color, size, and general health to impress females. Some males patrol, going on an active search for females. Others simply perch, sitting and waiting for a female to pass by.

Males do use pheromones, too, but they use them differently from the way females do. Male pheromones inhibit the female from flying and prepare her for mating. Then the male transfers a spermatophore to the female. This includes his sperm and several nutrients including fats, salts and nitrogen. The male may also leave behind an "anti-aphrodisiac" to ensure other males will not be attracted to the same female for up to two weeks to ensure that at least some of the female's eggs will be fertilized by the first suitor.

Life Cycle

Butterflies go through a complete metamorphosis that consists of four stages: egg, larva, pupa and adult.

Egg

Life for a butterfly begins with a tiny egg which depending on the species, may be spherical, hemispherical, ellipsoidal, spindle-shaped, lens-shaped, or rod-shaped. Soon after the egg is fertilized the female typically lays the eggs either singly or in masses on the host plant, which is the larvae food. Some species lay all their eggs on one plant while others use several locations. When eggs are laid in masses, some of the larvae may eat the unopened eggs as a first meal. A few butterflies lay their eggs while hovering in flight above the host plant.

Adult

The adult is the last or fourth stage in the metamorphosis or life cycle of the butterfly. The transformation is remarkable.

The lifespan for most adults ranges from a week to nine months, depending upon the species. The average is approxiately ten days.

Larva

Butterfly larvae are incredible eating machines. Over a period of fifteen to thirty days, larvae increase their size tremendously before they transform to the next stage. As a larva grows, it becomes too large for the outer covering and so must moult. The time intervals between moults are called instars. The number of instars that larvae have normally varies between three to five, depending upon the species.

Whether a larva or adult is poisonous or palatable often depends on what the larva eats.

The colors of many larvae species draw as little attention as possible. Other species may include bright warning colors or display false eyes to fool potential enemies.

Pupa

Once the larva has attained its maximum size, it will search for a suitable location to change into a pupa or chrysalis. With its last moult, it splits the cuticle (outer covering), shedding it to reveal the new soft pupa covering, which will soon harden. Externally, the pupa stage is one in which very little appears to change. Internally, however, many changes are occurring. The body of the larva changes into three sections: head, thorax and abdomen. Wings develop, waiting for the adult stage to become noticeable.

Doris longwing.

The Anatomy of the Butterfly

The body of the adult butterfly is comprised of three parts: head, thorax and abdomen.

Head

The eyes (see p. 15), the antennae and the mouthparts (see p. 16) are on the head.

Large tree nymph.

Thorax

Located between the head and abdomen, the thorax is responsible for locomotion or movement of the insect and consists of three short segments, each of which bears a pair of legs. In some species, the first pair of legs is very much reduced and may not appear to be present.

A pair of wings is also attached to each of the last two segments of the thorax. Besides being the means of flight, wings display the colors of a species. These colors will attract others of the same species and may provide camouflage or warning coloration as well. Color also plays an important part in regulating body temperature as darker colors absorb light while lighter colors reflect it.

Abdomen

The abdomen, which is usually covered with scales and hairs, houses organs of respiration, digestion, reproduction and excretion. Comprised of ten segments, it is the site of the genitalia (the external sex organs). The spiracles, the outer openings to the respiration system, are located along the sides of the abdomen.

Specialized Parts

The Eye

Butterflies have two sets of eyes. There are two simple eyes on the back of the head. No one knows what they are for. Compound eyes are for vision. The compound eyes are comprised of 12,000 to 17,000 simple eyes. Butterflies have the broadest visible spectrum known in the animal world. They can see from ultraviolet through the entire visible spectrum up to and including red. Unlike the human eye, which sees a broad picture, each simple eye views only a small area. The combined views give a complete picture. No wonder it is so difficult to approach a butterfly watching with at least 24,000 eyes!

The Mouthparts

A butterfly is designed to feed on liquid, especially nectar. The proboscis, composed of two half tubes held together by hooks to form a tube-like structure, acts like a straw. Muscles reduce the pressure at the base of the proboscis, creating suction to bring liquid food to the digestive system. When the proboscis is not used, it is stored in a coil under the head.

The Wings

Butterfly wings are comprised of a double membrane supported by veins. The forewings are often larger while the hind wings may display a variety of features including tails or grooves. Scales cover the wings and easily wear off as the butterfly ages.

Scales and Their Colors

A close look at a butterfly wing reveals a covering of tiny scales, essentially flattened bristles that overlap each other.
Pigments in the scales normally produce the colors in a butterfly's wings. Each type of pigment is responsible for a specific color. Melanin, for example, is the most common pigment and produces the blacks and grays found on many species.

Wings of scarlet Mormon.

Some butterflies exhibit an ultraviolet pattern that is visible to butterflies but not to man. Similar looking species, such as mimics, may display completely different ultraviolet patterns. Butterflies see the differences even though people cannot.

Several thin layers that filter light on the surface of wing scales can cause iridescence, like the rainbow effect seen in soap bubbles, most common in the blue and violet portion of the visible spectrum. Two spectacular examples are the common blue morpho (see p. 46) and emerald swallowtail (see p. 28).

Wing of emerald swallowtail.

Using This Book

All species found in this book have a common name and a scientific name. The current or most useful common name is included for each species. The scientific name is comprised of two Latin words: the genus (a grouping of species with common characteristics) and the species.

Maps indicate the approximate range of each species.

The butterflies in this book are organized in the evolutionary sequence that is commonly used in most references about butterflies. As entomologists (scientists who study insects) discover more about butterflies, they make changes to the classifications. For example, in 1991, longwings, believed to belong to a separate family, Helicondiiade, were found to be one of the brush-footed butterflies, family Nymphaliedae. There is still much to learn about butterflies.

THE BUTTERFLIES

Skippers (Family Hesperioidea)

Skippers are considered to be butterflies but they display some characteristics of moths. Unlike true butterflies, skippers have a thicker hairy body and hooked antennae. True butterfly antennae are filament-like with a bulbous end.

Skippers normally fold their wings in unique ways, depending on their group. They fly in a rapid and direct manner.

Two-barred Flasher

Astraptes fulgerator

OTHER NAMES: Blue flasher, flashing astraptes.
WINGSPAN: To 2 3/8 inches (6 cm).
FOODS: Adults feed on flower nectar and bird droppings.
RANGE: Argentina to Southern US (Texas).

The two-barred flasher gets its name from the two white bars on its upper wings, set off against a striking background of irides-cent blue. This butterfly favors forested areas near rivers and streams where adults feed on flower nectar and bird droppings and sometimes rest upside down under the shade of large leaves. Males often perch in the sun at a suitable vantage point waiting for females to be attracted by the pheromones coming from scent scales on the males' forewings.

19

King swallowtail (see p. 31).

Swallowtails
& Birdwings (Family Papilionidae)

Swallowtails, medium or large in size, have interesting wings with unique veining patterns. Often they have one or two long tail-like extensions on the bottom of the hindwing.

Living primarily in Australia and Papua New Guinea, birdwings are the largest butterflies. The largest is the Alexandra. The first specimen collected was felled by a shotgun blast. Now that's a large butterfly!

Tailed Jay
Graphium agamemnon

OTHER NAMES: Green jay, green triangle, green spotted triangle; Formerly *Zetides agamemnon*.
WINGSPAN: To 4 inches (10 cm).
FOODS: Adults feed on flower nectar.
RANGE: Northern India to Australia

A common species, the tailed jay is found year-round. The scientific name for this rapid flyer likely harkens back to Agamemnon, the great king of ancient Greece. Several of its common names are taken from its bright green coloration that matches the sun-dappled forest of its habitat, where the males sometimes congregate at seepages. We can tell the males from the females because the males have longer tails on their hindwings.

21

Pink Cattleheart
Parides iphidamas

OTHER NAME: *P. iphidamus*.
WINGSPAN: To 3 1/3 inches
(8.5 cm).
FOODS: Adults feed on
flower nectar and it is believed that some adults feed on pollen.
RANGE: Mexico to South America.

Cattleshearts get their name from their tapered blood-red spots
that resemble miniature hearts. This species flutters its wings
continually while visiting flowers. The adults are poisonous since
the larvae feed on a toxic vine (*Aristolochia* sp.).

In courtship, the male hovers over the female. If she approves of
her suitor, she will slowly flutter her wings favorably. If not, she
closes her wings. When the male is suc-
cessful in mating with the female,
he leaves a sphragis (mating
plug) covering the tip of the
female's abdomen, ensuring she
will not mate again until the
sphragis disintegrates.

22

Male.

Orchard Swallowtail
Papilio aegeus

OTHER NAMES: Orchard butterfly, citrus swallowtail.
WINGSPAN: To 5 inches (12 cm).
FOODS: Adults feed on flower nectar.
RANGE: E. Australia, Indonesia and New Guinea.

The large orchard swallowtail flies year-round and is wary and difficult to approach. It has adapted well to the introduction of citrus groves in Australia. In the early instars of the larval stage it avoids detection by predators because it resembles bird droppings. In the final instar, all swallowtail larvae emit a pungent secretion of a butyric acid compound that irritates and repels potential predators including birds, mammals, ants, spiders and wasps.

Males are black overall with a red spot and white or cream crescents. Females have more red on their wings.

23

Common Mormon
Papilio polytes

OTHER NAME: *Princeps polytes*.
WINGSPAN: To 4 inches (10 cm).
FOODS: Adults feed on flower nectar.
RANGE: Southeast Asia.

Mormon is the common name for many black swallowtails that often have conspicuous tails on their hindwings. The sexes of this species are very different in coloration. Females display crimson on their hindwings while males display only white bands. Neither sex has any red on its body. Fifteen subspecies are visible in the female only. Some have tails on their hindwings and others do not. Two of these subspecies mimic poisionous swallowtails occurring in the same range: the crimson rose swallowtail (*Pachliopta hector*) and common rose swallowtail (*Pachliopta aristolochia*).

Male.

This strong flier is often found near the orange and lime planta-tions that provide food for the larvae. On sunny days, males hover above blossoms.

Scarlet Mormon
Papilio rumanzovia

Male.

OTHER NAMES: Crimson Mormon, scarlet swallowtail; *Menelaides rumanzovius, M. rumanzovia*.
WINGSPAN: To 6 inches (15 cm).
FOODS: Adults feed on flower nectar.
RANGE: Philippines.

Like many other butterfly species, the scarlet Mormon female takes on a different appearance in each of its subspecies while all the males look the same. The striking wings of both the males and females have vivid red undersides. The upper sides of the female's wings, always primarily black, have various red and white markings. The larvae feed on leaves of citrus plants.

26

Emerald Swallowtail
Papilio palinurus

OTHER NAMES: Banded peacock, Burmese banded peacock, moss peacock, green moss peacock; *Princeps palinurus*.
WINGSPAN: To 3 ½ inches (9 cm).
FOODS: Adults feed on flower nectar.
RANGE: Southeast Asia.

A true jewel on the wing, the emerald swallowtail flies so high in the forest canopy people seldom see it. The magnificent emerald iridescence comes from two structural colors that are placed extremely close together. Yellow at the bottom of minute cavities in the wing scales and blue along the edge of the scales produce the emerald green we see. We view color on TV in the same way. This method of combining color has been patented and may in fact be used for anti-counterfeiting measures for credit cards, banknotes and travelers' checks. It is amazing to think that the origin of the idea came from the wing of a butterfly.

Male.

Mocker Swallowtail
Papilio dardanus

WINGSPAN: To 4 ½ inches (11 cm).
FOODS: Adults feed on Nectar.
RANGE: Africa.

The mocker swallowtail is a common forest species in Africa. It is named for the fact that the females

One of the many female forms.

mimic the coloration of several different toxic butterflies. The females of some subspecies have tails while others do not. Females may be black and white, black and orange, orange and black or other combinations. Males have tails and their coloration is uniform throughout the range. This species has been the focus of several studies to learn more about its mimicry.

King Swallowtail
Papilio thoas

OTHER NAMES: South American giant swallowtail, giant swallowtail, citrus swallowtail, Thoas swallowtail.
WINGSPAN: To 5 inches (12.5 cm).
FOODS: Adults feed on flower nectar.
RANGE: South America to Southern United States (Texas).

This large, beautiful species visits flowers year round at tropical forest edges and high in the rain forest canopy. It is frequently observed sipping mud. A strong and rapid flight is characteristic for this solitary species that very rarely strays as far north as Kansas and Oklahoma. The larva of the king swallowtail, like several others of the swallowtail clan, uses a great camouflage technique: It resembles a bird dropping.

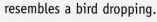

31

Velvet Rose Swallowtail
Pachliopta kotzebuea

OTHER NAMES: Kotzebuea swallowtail; *Atrophaneura kotzebuea*.
WINGSPAN: To 5 inches (13 cm).
FOODS: Adults feed on flower nectar.
RANGE: Philippines.

The exquisite velvet rose swallowtail has jet-black velvety wings with prominent tails. The body is also jet-black while the head and tip of the abdomen have a touch of red pigment. This common species depends on the dwindling rainforest that is being cleared for development. Unfortunately, rainforest is being removed around the world at an alarming rate.

Gold-rim Swallowtail
Battus polydamas

OTHER NAMES: Gold-rim, tailless swallowtail; *B. polydamus.*
WINGSPAN: To 4 ½ inches (11 cm).
FOODS: Adults feed on flower nectar and mud.
RANGE: South America to Southern United States.

The gold-rim swallowtail, which does not in fact have a tail, lives in disturbed areas on both the Pacific and Atlantic slopes of Central and South America. Caterpillars feed on the leaves and flowers of pipe vines and, as a result, the gold rim swallowtail is distasteful to birds. It is interesting to note that the larvae of this species also feed on tropical plants used as ornamentals in more temperate regions, a fact that likely helps to extend their range occasionally as far as north as Kentucky and Missouri. In Brazil, the average lifespan of the adult is one week although some gold-rim swallowtails live to 28 days.

33

Cairns Birdwing
Troides priamus

Male.

OTHER NAME: *Ornithoptera priamus*.
WINGSPAN: To 8 inches (20 cm).
FOODS: Larvae feed on Dutchman's pipe vines. Adults feed on wildflower nectar.
RANGE: North-east Australia.

Striking does not adequately describe the colors found in bird-wing butterflies. With wings rivaling the size of birds wings, these are also the largest butterflies in the world. The female Cairns bird-wing is somber colored and much larger than the spectacular male.

34

Female forelegs hold chemical receptors that help to find food plants by tasting leaves. Sense organs at the tip of the female abdomen locate leaves suitable for larvae to feed on. Dutchman's pipe, a poisonous vine being lost to urban development, farming and forestry, is food for the larvae of this species. The poison is passed on to adult butterflies. All birdwing butterflies are dwindling in the wild primarily due to the loss of their habitat.

Female.

Male.

Orange-barred sulfur (see p. 38).

Whites & Sulphurs (Family Pieridae)

The majority of members of this family are white or yellow in color, as their family name implies. Individuals in this group have forked "feet". When viewed in ultraviolet light, the wings of many species produce specific patterns to help identify potential mates. The males of several species are sexually dimorphic (colored differently) from the females.

The Great Orange Tip
Hebomoia glaucippe

OTHER NAME: White and orange-brown tip.
WINGSPAN: To 4 inches (10 cm).
FOODS: Adults feed on nectar and drink from wet patches.
RANGE: Southeast Asia.

This wary fast flier prefers areas of high rainfall. The largest of the whites found in Southeast Asia is quite a sight while flying or holding its wings half-closed as it does while feeding. The color pattern changes dramatically when the great orange tip closes its wings to rest, revealing the cryptic (camouflage) coloration of its hindwing underside that closely resembles a brown leaf, producing a sharp contrast to the bright white and orange colors of the upper surface of the wing.

37

Orange-barred Sulfur
Phoebis philea

OTHER NAMES:
Apricot sulfur;
Phoebus philea.
WINGSPAN: To 4
inches (10 cm).
FOODS: Adults
feed on nectar.
RANGE: Brazil to
southern United
States (Florida).

The orange-barred
sulfur, like most
sulfurs, closes its
wings above its
body while rest-
ing, effectively
hiding the red-
orange bar pres-
ent on the upper
surface that gives

this species its common name. Various birds find this colorful
species edible so it depends on its strong and fast flight to elude
its enemies. Females are much larger than males, laying their
eggs singly on their host plants. Instead of eating leaves like
most caterpillars, the larva eats flowers and pulls down the tip
of a leaf of the food plant to make a tent to hide in during the
daytime. This species, like many other butterflies, lives in several
different habitats: temperate forest, temperate rainforest, and
tropical rainforest.

Leafwing (see p. 72).

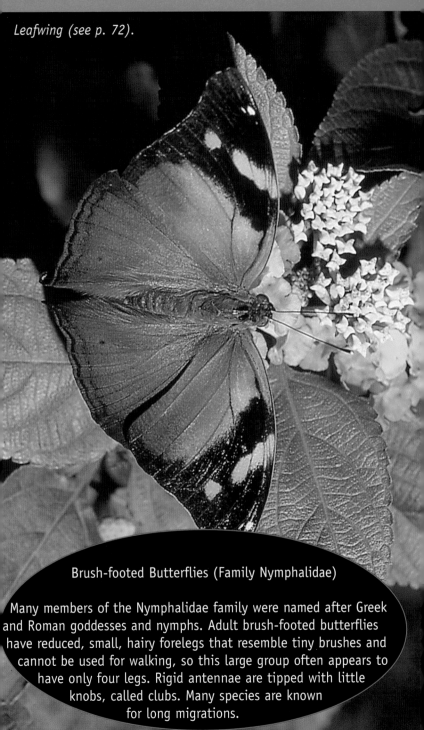

Brush-footed Butterflies (Family Nymphalidae)

Many members of the Nymphalidae family were named after Greek and Roman goddesses and nymphs. Adult brush-footed butterflies have reduced, small, hairy forelegs that resemble tiny brushes and cannot be used for walking, so this large group often appears to have only four legs. Rigid antennae are tipped with little knobs, called clubs. Many species are known for long migrations.

Monarch
Danaus plexippus

OTHER NAMES: Common tiger, wanderer, black veined brown.
WINGSPAN: To 4 ⅞ inches (12.4 cm).
FOODS: Adults feed on flower nectar.
RANGE: South America to Southern Canada. Also present in Australia, Hawaii and other Pacific Islands.

The spectacular migration of the monarch is familiar to many. In North America, thousands of monarchs migrate in large aggregations from their increasingly threatened southern over-wintering sites in Mexico and California to sites as far north as Southern Canada. Other monarchs living in tropical areas appear to make altitude changes rather than latitudinal migrations. In Australia, the monarch does not migrate. Its instinct to aggregate draws large groups together to roost in trees at night.

Larvae feed on the poisonous milkweed. As a result both the larva and adult are poisonous. Predators learn quickly to avoid the distinctive monarch colors. The viceroy butterfly (*Limenitis archippus*) mimics the monarch in North America in order to gain protection from predators.

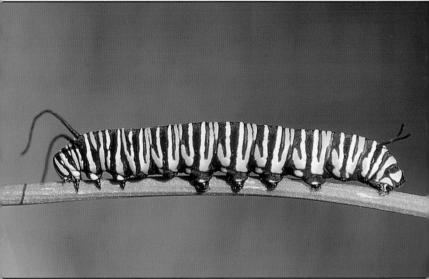

Mullerian Mimicry

The monarch is a well-known poisonous model for mimicry. For many years scientists believed that the viceroy was an edible butterfly whose protection from predators depended to some extent on its being colored the same as the monarch. Recent research shows that the viceroy is also poisonous. Since both the monarch and the viceroy are inedible, both are protected by this example of Mullerian mimicry (see p. 10).

Small Wood Nymph
Ideopsis juventa

OTHER NAMES: Formerly *Danaus juventa, Idiopsis juventa*.
WINGSPAN: To 3 3/8 inches (8.5 cm).
FOODS: Adults feed on nectar.
RANGE: Southeast Asia.

This species is found on many islands within its limited range and each island has developed its own variety or subspecies. The color and pattern of both sexes are similar. This species is unpalatable to birds and other local species copy its distinctive coloration. Little is known about the natural history of this species.

Large Tree Nymph
Idea leuconoe

OTHER NAMES: Paper kite, white tree nymph, rice paper; *Idea leucone*.
WINGSPAN: To 6 inches (15 cm).
FOODS: Adults feed on flower nectar.
RANGE: Southeast Asia.

With slow deliberate wing beats, the beautiful, large tree nymph glides just below the forest canopy in coastal regions. The thin translucent wings give this species the name rice paper. It is the largest of the milkweed butterflies (subfamily Danainae) and is believed to be distasteful to predators. The jewel-like pupae of this species are bright gold.

Common Glasswing
Greta oto

OTHER NAME: Glasswing.
WINGSPAN: To 2 ¼ inches (5.8 cm).
FOODS: Adults feed on flower nectar.
RANGE: Panama to Mexico.

The common glasswing is one of about 400 species of clear-wings worldwide, many of which are very similar in appearance. This is one of the most common species found in Central America where adults are present throughout the year. The transparent areas of the wings have no scales. Common glasswings normally travel about 8 miles (12 km) per day on migration, but one individual was found to move over 26.4 miles (40 km) in one day. This species lives in low-lying Pacific rainforests to elevations of 4950' (1500 m). Members of this dainty group commonly rest with their wings in an upright position.

Consul Leaf Mimic
Consul electra

OTHER NAME: *Archaeopreponia meander.*
WINGSPAN: To 3 ¾ inches (9.5 cm).
FOODS: Adults feed on flower nectar.
RANGE: Mexico to Panama.

The consul leaf mimic looks so much like a leaf that its presence often goes unnoticed. It rests with its wings in the upright position, so the upper side of the wings is normally hidden from view. For about an hour in the morning, males select a perch in the forest canopy and chase away most butterflies that venture nearby. Females are active at forest edges around noon.

45

Common Blue Morpho
Morpho peleides

OTHER NAME: Blue morpho.
WINGSPAN: To 5 inches (12 cm).
FOODS: Adults feed on fruit.
RANGE: Columbia and Venezuela to Mexico.

Its size and color makes a first glimpse of a common blue morpho a sight to remember. It is often found flying along rivers, at forest edges, and in plantations from sea level to elevations of 5940' (1,800 m), where its "floppy flight" takes it in a somewhat zigzag fashion. Males patrol for females from morning to midday while the larger females, which have a wider black margin on their wings, are normally active only at midday. Adults do not feed on flower nectar, but rather on rotting fruit.

46

When resting, they keep their wings closed above their bodies. The resulting brown display attracts little attention. A row of eyespots present on the underside of their wings helps to identify this species.

Cream Owl Butterfly

Caligo memnon

OTHER NAMES: Tawny owl butterfly, Memnon's owl.
WINGSPAN: To 6 3/8 inches (16 cm).
FOODS: Larvae feed on the leaves of bananas and other large leafed plants.
RANGE: Central and South America.

Female laying eggs.

A large cream-colored patch on the upper inside surface of the forewings gives the cream owl butterfly its common name. When closed, the upper wings also reveal a light-colored section.

The cream owl butterfly is a common species found in drier areas of its range along the Pacific slope unlike its close relatives, the giant owl butterfly and the banded owl butterfly (see opposite page) that prefer wetter rain forests. The cream owl butterfly also survives in severely disturbed agricultural areas. The life cycle of the cream owl butterfly can be found on page 12.

SIMILAR SPECIES

Giant Owl Butterfly
Caligo eurilochus

WINGSPAN: To 7 inches (18 cm).
FOODS: Adults feed on rotting fruit including bananas.
RANGE: Central and South America.

The owl butterflies get their name from the large eyespots, which look like owl eyes, found on the underside of their hindwings. When the underside of the hindwing is brown, you can be sure you have found a giant owl butterfly. Unlike most butterflies, this species is crepuscular or active at dusk and dawn and as a result they are sometimes mistakenly thought to be bats in flight. Their larvae are considered a pest in banana plantations.

Banded Owl Butterfly
Caligo atreus

WINGSPAN: To 6 5/8 inches (17 cm).
FOODS: Adults feed on rotting fruits.
RANGE: Central and South America.

This large species lives in the rain forests of both the Pacific and Atlantic slopes. Like all species of owl butterflies, it prefers to fly at dusk and dawn, as do their owl counterparts in the bird world.

When the wings of the banded owl butterfly are closed, the outer edge of both wings display a bright yellowish band. The upper surface of the forewing boasts a beautiful blue and the hindwing sports an impressive bright yellow band.

The larvae of owl butterflies are left untouched by raiding army ants. Research is needed to determine why.

Red Lacewing
Cethosia biblis

OTHER NAME: Hong Kong lacewing.
WINGSPAN: To 3 ½ inches (9 cm).
FOODS: Adults feed on flower nectar.
RANGE: Southeast Asia.

The red lacewing lives in the hills of Southeast Asia. The female is gray. The upper surface of the male is red. Its bright colors warn predators that it tastes awful. Larvae feed on poisonous plants in the passion vine family. The larvae are strikingly colored with long barbed spines believed to sting or itch those that contact them. Adults are normally found flying near their food plants. Here, males await the emergence of females for mating. There are 4 or 5 generations during the year. Since people sometimes see tattered individuals, some believe that certain individuals in this species are long-lived.

50

Leopard Lacewing
Cethosia cyane

WINGSPAN: To 3 ¾ inches (9.5 cm).
FOODS: Adults feed on flower nectar.
RANGE: Southeast Asia.

The striking lacy features of the leopard lacewing and the red lacewing (previous species) give them their names and make identification easy. Not only do they have delicate lacy patterns on the underside of their wings, but they also have indentations along the wing edges, increasing the lacy effect. Upper surfaces of the wings of female leopard lacewings are pale green-white. Little is known about the natural history of this species.

51

Tiger Longwing
Dryadula phaetusa

OTHER NAMES: Banded orange, orange tiger, banded orange heliconian.
WINGSPAN: To 3 ½ inches (8.9 cm).
FOODS: Adults feed on flower nectar.
RANGE: Mexico to Brazil.

Orange wings with black stripes give the tiger longwing its common name. Males are brighter colored and have distinct black stripes, while females have blurry black stripes. Adults feed on flower nectar and bird droppings. This species' flight is like a dragonfly. Sometimes the tiger longwing roosts gregariously on grass at night. Very little is known about its natural history.

52

Isabella Tiger Longwing
Eueides isabella

OTHER NAME: Isabella's heliconian.
WINGSPAN: To 3 ½ inches (9 cm).
FOODS: Adults feed on flower nectar.
RANGE: Mexico to Brazil and the West Indies.

The Isabella tiger longwing begins life as a lone egg on a passion vine, its food, either on a tendril (clasping stem) or on the underside of a leaf. After hatching, the larva begins feeding on its host plant to gain enough size to molt several times. Passion vines fight back by producing egg-like buds on their leaves to deter females from laying real eggs on the same leaf. Some vines also produce sugary secretions that attract ants and protect the vines from young caterpillars.

The adults are poisonous since they feed on poisonous plants as larvae. Year-round, adults roost alone on the undersides of leaves. Males actively patrol for females.

53

Orange Julia
Dryas iulia

OTHER NAMES: Orange long wing, Julia, flambeau; *Dryas julia*.
WINGSPAN: To 3 ½ inches (9 cm).
FOODS: Adults feed on flower nectar.
RANGE: South America to Southern United States.

Distinctive bright orange elongated wings identify the alert orange Julia, noted for its dragonfly-like flight. Adults are present year-round at low elevations where they favor red or blue flowers. Males often sample mud. A male may spend the entire day seeking a female. When he finds one, he fans her with his wings to ensure that she detects the scent from his scent scales. If she is impressed, she emits her scent, signaling her acceptance. She then vibrates and eventually mates.

Zebra Longwing
Heliconius charitonia

OTHER NAMES: Zebra long wing, zebra; *H. charitonius*.
WINGSPAN: To 3 ¾ inches (9.5 cm).
FOODS: Adults feed on flower nectar.
RANGE: Peru to Southern United States.

Unlike other species in the Heliconius group, the distinctive adult zebra longwing is unable to feed on pollen so it does not live as long as these closely related species (see the postman p. 58). Zebra longwing larvae feed on host plants that are poisonous to other Heliconius species. The adult commonly migrates for 200 miles (300 km) and on occasion to 500 miles (750 km) with a slow ghostly flight. This species roosts in groups of 70 individuals or more. The male, like the small postman (p. 60), mates with the female before she has broken out of her pupa casing. He then adds a repellent pheromone to her stink clubs to repel other males.

Doris Longwing
Heliconius doris

OTHER NAME: Doris.
WINGSPAN: To 4 inches (10 cm).
FOODS: Adults are thought to feed on both pollen and nectar.
RANGE: Amazon Basin to Mexico.

Heliconius butterflies are diverse and need more research. The color range of this stunning species is highly variable and includes yellow, red, blue, green or mixtures of these colors. Unlike most other species in the Heliconius clan, the Doris longwing does not have any mimics. It does, however, have a different number of chromosomes from others in its genus, and behaves differently from other species within the same genus (*Heliconius*).

Postman
Heliconius melpomene

OTHER NAMES: Crimson-patched longwing, red passion-flower butterfly
WINGSPAN: To 3 ¼ inches (8 cm).
FOODS: Adults feed on pollen and nectar.
RANGE: Brazil to Mexico.

Heliconius butterflies are also called passion vine butterflies. Their larvae are one of few butterflies that feed on the passion vine, a plant that contains cyanide and makes the larvae poisonous. The adults produce their own cyanide to make themselves poisonous to predators. Most butterflies live for a mere 10 days. The postman is able to live 25 times longer than most butterflies (up to 9 months) by feeding on pollen.

58

The postman has been the focus of many scientific studies for decades. To identify the postman, check the underside of the lower wing for 3 red dots. On the upper side of the wing, the red band lacks a distinct edge and looks smudged.

How the Postman Got Its Name
It feeds on a series of flowers and repeats these feeding stops on a daily basis much like a postman delivers the mail, house-to-house, at about the same time every day.

Small Postman

Heliconius erato

OTHER NAME: Crimson-patched long-wing, red passion-flower butterfly.
WINGSPAN: To 3 1/8 inches (8 cm).
FOODS: Adults feed on the pollen of a wide variety of species.
RANGE: Mexico to Brazil.

This species mimics the postman (see p. 59), another poisonous species. To identify the small post-man, look for 4 red dots on the underside of the lower wing. The upper side of the wing displays a red band with a distinct edge. The male of the small postman mates with the female before she has broken out of her pupa casing. The male then deposits a chemical repellant on the female's abdomen to deter other males.

The adult small postman feeds on the pollen from a wide variety of flowers so it is able to live for several months using this concentrated protein. This species is the most common Heliconius found in Costa Rica.

Black and White Longwing
Heliconius cydno

OTHER NAMES: Blue and white longwing, black and white helicon, cydno helicon.
WINGSPAN: To 3 ½ inches (9 cm).
FOODS: Adults feed on flower pollen.
RANGE: Ecuador to Mexico.

The black and white longwing is a poisonous species with a fluttery and deliberate flight that advertises its warning coloration and poisonous properties. In the forests of Ecuador, a flycatcher (a insectivorous bird) was observed looping around a black and white longwing to avoid it in order to capture a moth. The abdominal glands of this species produce a distinctive, pungent smell.

61

Eleuchia Longwing
Heliconius eleuchia

WINGSPAN: To 3 ½ inches (9 cm).
FOODS: Adults feed on flowers and possibly pollen.
RANGE: Central and northern South America.

The Eleuchia longwing is a beautiful but uncommon species living in a restricted area along the Atlantic slope at elevations between 330' to 2310' (100 to 700 m). This species is often observed in the morning, flying along rivers and on the tops of ridges. In some areas, males have been observed mating with females prior to emerging from their pupae stage. Little else is known about its natural history.

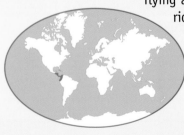

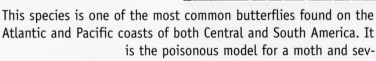

Golden Helicon
Heliconius hecale

OTHER NAME: Tiger longwing.
WINGSPAN: To 3 inches (8 cm).
FOODS: Adults feed on flower pollen.
RANGE: South America to Mexico.

This species is one of the most common butterflies found on the Atlantic and Pacific coasts of both Central and South America. It is the poisonous model for a moth and several unrelated butterflies that live within the same range and survive using the poisonous reputation of the golden helicon. The golden helicon is believed to be migratory.

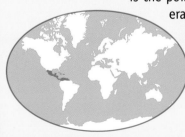

Sara Longwing
Heliconius sara

OTHER NAMES: Small blue grecian, blue heliconid.
WINGSPAN: To 2 ⅛ inches (5.5 cm).
FOODS: Adults feed on flower pollen.
RANGE: Brazil to Mexico.

The Sara longwing lives at the forest edge or in secondary rain forests at elevations from sea level to 2310' (700 m) on both the Pacific and Atlantic slopes of Central and South America. In groups of up to 40 individuals, this small species roosts overnight low to the ground near streams.

Cyaniris Bluewing
Myscelia cyaniris

OTHER NAMES: Blue wave, banded purple wing.
WINGSPAN: To 2 ½ inches (6.5 cm).
FOODS: Adults feed on rotting fruit.
RANGE: Peru to Mexico.

The cyaniris bluewing is often found near the food plants of its larvae. At rest the adult folds its wings, forewing behind the hindwing, forming a neat triangle when viewed from the side. Considering the bright iridescent blue of the upper wing surface, the reduced visibility of its tight fold is a great advantage in avoiding potential predators.

65

Brown Clipper
Parthenos sylvia philippensis

OTHER NAME: Clipper.
WINGSPAN: To 4 inches (10 cm).
FOODS: Adults feed on flower nectar.
RANGE: Philippines.

The brown clipper, a strong flier, lives in lowland jungle from 1,000' to 3,000' (300 - 900 m) in areas of heavy rainfall and spends its time high in the canopy or in congregations at the wet edges of streams. In the canopy it rests with outstretched wings on a leaf. From this base it makes many other shorter flights to surrounding areas.

66

Blue Clipper
Parthenos sylvia lilacinus

OTHER NAME: Clipper.
WINGSPAN: To 4 inches (10 cm).
FOODS: Adults feed on flower nectar.
RANGE: Malay peninsula.

Physical barriers such as islands or mountains can create isolated populations of a species. Sometimes this can cause a color change in one population and a new subspecies. For example, the main color of both the forewings and hindwings of the blue clipper is lilac blue rather than the brown of the brown clipper (see previous page).

Red Cracker
Hamadryas amphinome

OTHER NAME: Blue cracker.
WINGSPAN: To 3 3/8 inches (8.5 cm).
FOODS: Adults feed on rotting fruit.
RANGE: Argentina to Central Mexico and Cuba.

This species is named for the cracking or clicking sound, created by a specialized mechanism found on the wing, made as it darts about. Color also adds to its name. The red cracker displays a red patch on its underside of the hind wing. Due to its upper coloration, it is also known as the blue cracker. Adults often rest on the trunks of trees with their heads facing downward and their wings held open. Before dark they gather to roost together on a single tree or shrub. This species occasionally strays from its normal range into the southern United States.

Neotropical Mosaic
Colobura dirce

OTHER NAME: Zebra butterfly.
WINGSPAN: To 3 inches (7.6 cm).
FOODS: Adults feed on tree sap, rotting fruit, carrion and dung.
RANGE: South America to Mexico and the West Indies.

This common and widespread species is present year-round but never in high numbers. Each day around noon, the Neotropical mosaic locates a suitable tree trunk to perch on and rest with its head pointed downward. In urban areas, wet laundry attracts this species. The pattern of zebra butterfly wings is an excellent example of disruptive coloration that breaks up the outline of the insect, no matter what the background is.

69

Malachite
Siproeta stelenes

OTHER NAME: Pearly malachite.
WINGSPAN: To 4 inches (10 cm).
FOODS: Adults feed on flower nectar, rotting fruit, bird droppings and carrion.
RANGE: Brazil to Southern United States (Florida and Texas).

The malachite butterfly is named after malachite, a green mineral that contains copper compounds. This common butterfly feeds all day on a wide variety of foods from orchards and occasionally domestic gardens. Males perch in forest openings to wait for females, or patrol for females with a slow and somewhat floating flight. Adults roost communally in small groups under large leaves.

This species has two or three broods each year, laying its green eggs singly. The larvae are very dark velvety green with prominent horns.

70

Female.

Great Eggfly
Hypolimnas bolina

OTHER NAMES: Greater egg-fly,
great egg fly, common eggfly,
blue moon butterfly;
Hypolimnis bolina.
WINGSPAN: To 3 inches (8 cm).
FOODS: Adults feed on flower
nectar.
RANGE: India, Ceylon, Burma
and Australia.

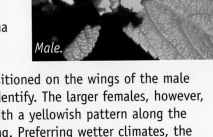

Male.

Brilliant blue oval spots positioned on the wings of the male
make this species easy to identify. The larger females, however,
look completely different with a yellowish pattern along the
upper edge of the lower wing. Preferring wetter climates, the
great eggfly, sometimes seen with tat-
tered wings, is long-lived.
Pugnacious males often remain
at the same resting spot for
days at a time, spending much
of their time chasing away all
butterflies that venture too close.

71

Leafwing
Doleschallia bisaltide

OTHER NAMES: Australian leafwing, autumn leaf; *D. basaltide*.
WINGSPAN: To 3 3/8 inches (8.5 cm).
FOODS: Adults feed on flower nectar.
RANGE: Southeast Asia.

Preferring shade or the dappled sunlight of thick jungle, the leafwing often rests with its wings folded in the upright position giving it a striking resemblance to a leaf. No doubt, avian predators would have a difficult time discovering this species. While it sips nectar or feeds on fermenting fruit, it may open its wings to reveal its tawny upper wing pattern. The lower surface of the hindwing sports two small eyespots. Adults live for eight weeks or longer.

Male.

Grecian Shoemaker
Catonephele numilia

WINGSPAN: To 3 inches (7.5 cm).
FOODS: Adults feed on rotting fruit.
RANGE: South America to Mexico.

The male and female Grecian shoemakers look so dissimilar that they appear to be two separate species. Since this distinctive species prefers a solitary existence in shady areas including the rain forest sub canopy and similar sites, it often goes undetected in wet forests from sea level to 3,300' (1,000 m) on both the Atlantic and Pacific slopes. Males may be observed waiting for females in patches of sunlight, perched on tree trunks in the morning until the early afternoon. While feeding on fallen fruit, its folded wings blend perfectly with its surroundings.

CONSERVATION

Habitat loss is the main cause of changes in the butterfly world. Previously inaccessible tropical rainforest is cut for cattle production. Loss of rainforest has become a major global concern for more than butterflies. Many invertebrates and vertebrates are in trouble. We must stop the present course now and begin to preserve the remaining rain forests.

The future of butterflies, and indeed all wildlife species, lies with the protection of suitable habitats so all species have a chance for long-term survival.

BUTTERFLY FARMING

In various locations around the globe, butterfly farming has become an innovative way for locals to help their local economy, to provide a valid reason for maintaining local forests, and to conserve butterflies. A single female butterfly in the wild may lay several hundred eggs of which only 4 may survive. If instead, these eggs are placed in the controlled conditions of a butterfly farm, perhaps 75% will survive. In butterfly farming, some butterflies are returned to the wild, some are sold, and some are kept for breeding. Many butterfly species benefit from such farming.

Butterfly farmers in Belize, Costa Rica, El Salvador, Papua New Guinea, Thailand and other countries have learned a great deal while breeding several species in captivity. Farmers provide a variety of live species to butterfly houses around the world. As a result, the public, most of whom would never be able to see the butterflies in the wild, can view a wide selection of butterflies from around the world in butterfly gardens and conservatories.

GLOSSARY

Batesian mimicry: where an edible species mimics the coloration of an inedible or poisonous species to gain protection from its coloration.

chrysalis: the pupa stage of a butterfly that follows the larva stage.

crepuscular: active at dawn and or at dusk.

diurnal: active in the day.

instar: developmental stage of an insect between molts.

larva: the developmental stage between the egg and pupa.

larvae: the plural of larva.

metamorphosis: a developmental change during the life cycle of an organism.

Mullerian mimicry: a poisonous species mimics the colors of another poisonous species.

nocturnal: active during the night.

pheromone: chemical compound produced to create a behavioral response by others of the same species.

proboscis: straw-like tongue.

pupa: the developmental stage of an insect between the larva and adult.

pupae: plural of pupa.

scent scales: modified scales capable of producing chemical compounds that act as pheromones.

spermatophore: a package containing sperm, placed in the females body by the male.

sphragis: a mating plug produced by the male to cover the end of a females abdomen to prevent the female from mating with another male.

stink clubs: small projections on females butterflies emitting noxious fumes to repel male butterflies.

ACKNOWLEDGMENTS

I would like to thank the following individuals who assisted with this project.

Audrey Owen for her excellent editing.

Mark Deering for the identification of several species of butter-flies.

The skilled photographers who provided additional photos. Their names appear below.

PHOTO CREDITS

BIBLIOGRAPHY

Dickens, Michael. 1972. The World of Butterflies. The Macmillan Company, New York, NY

DeVries, P. J. 1987. The Butterflies of Costa Rica and their Natural History. Papilionidae, Pieridae, Nymphalidae. Princeton University Press, Princeton, New Jersey.

Preston-Mafham, R. and K. 1988. Butterflies of the World. Facts on File, Inc. New York, NY.

Sbordoni, Valerio and Forestiero, Saverio. 1998. Butterflies of the World. Firefly Books. New York, NY.

Scoble, Malcolm J. 1995. The Lepidoptera: Form, Function and Diversity. Oxford University Press & Natural History Museum (London), New York, NY

Scott, James A. 1986. The Butterflies of North America: A Natural History and Field Guide. Stanford University Press. Stanford, CA

Shappert, Phil. 2000. A World of Butterflies: Their Lives, Behavior and Future. Key Porter Books. Toronto, ON

Son, G. Van. 1970 (reprint). The Butterflies of Southern Africa: Part I Papilionicae and Pieridae. Memoir No. 3, October 1949, Swets & Zeitlinger N.V., Amsterdam, Netherlands

Wynter-Blyth, M.A. 1957. Butterflies of the Indian Region. Bombay Natural History Society, Mumbai.

INDEX

About the Author

Duane Sept is a biologist, freelance writer and professional photographer. His biological work has included research on various wildlife species and service as a park naturalist. His award-winning photographs have been published internationally, in displays and in books, magazines and other publications, for clients that include BBC Wildlife, Parks Canada, Nature Canada, National Wildlife Federation and World Wildlife Fund.

Today Duane brings a wealth of information to the public as an author, in much the same way he has inspired hundreds of visitors to Canada's parks. His published books include The Beachcomber's Guide to Seashore Life in the Pacific Northwest (Harbour Publishing), Common Birds of British Columbia (Calypso Publishing) and Common Wildflowers of British Columbia (Calypso Publishing). He lives on the Sunshine Coast of British Columbia with his family.